PSALMS FROM THE HEART:
Devotions of Triumph

Dr. Lakisha Foxworth

Psalms from the Heart: Devotions of Triumph

Copyright © 2014 Lakisha Foxworth

ISBN 978-1-939614-37-7

Unless otherwise noted, all Scripture quotations are taken from the Holy Bible, King James Version.

Dedication

I dedicate this book to my sisters in Christ.
They know who they are; they know the
struggle all too well.

To those who suffer in silence, I give voice.
Be encouraged!
The One who has overcome the world is in you.
Therefore, you have the power to overcome!

TABLE OF CONTENTS

Foreword....vi

Introduction....vii

For the Mind....1

For the Soul....10

His Promises....17

Praise....36

The Word....42

Foreword

By Pastor Lisa Elliott
Center of Hope International

Dr. Lakisha Foxworth is an outstanding author, speaker and counselor. I've been blessed to pastor and mentor such an incredible woman with an unbelievable testimony. This book is a powerful tool for you to overcome difficult obstacles in your life.

As you open this Spirit-inspired book, you'll discover truths that will help set you free and move you forward into God's will for your life.

Introduction

In my first book, *I'm Coming Out: A Story of Triumph over Sickness, Dis-ease and Abuse*, I shared about my struggle to overcome a past of verbal, emotional and sexual abuse, which ultimately led to my becoming infected with HIV. The story unfolds from the discovery of my status to significant physical, mental and spiritual battles. It ended with my profession of healing through Jesus Christ.

Psalms from the Heart is a collection of Scriptures and meditations I selected to lean upon during some of the most difficult times in my personal journey toward triumph – triumph over sickness and disease, pain and strife, and triumph from a past of unconscionable abuse. My hope is that you'll find something heart-touching in these devotions to help you triumph over your own enemies.

For the Mind...

> *"O Lord, thou hast searched me and known me, thou knowest my downsitting and mine uprising, thou understandest my thoughts afar off."*
> PSALMS 139:1-2

God sees us the way no one else can. He sees our potential, our flaws, strengths and weaknesses. He knows it all because He manufactured us; therefore, He's the only one who can truly fix all that goes wrong with us. He's able to fix us physically, mentally, emotionally, and spiritually. He can and will do it. He's able to put us Humpty Dumptys back together again, and it's amazing that He longs to do just that for us.

After receiving a diagnosis like HIV at the prime of my life (age 18), it's safe to say I was broken. It seemed I'd never feel whole again. When I couldn't understand myself, my thoughts held me captive to my situation and it seemed I couldn't gain clarity, no matter how hard I tried. I found solace in this Scripture that even though I don't get it, I serve a God who does. Sometimes just knowing that someone gets it – and gets you – is enough to propel you forward. ♥

> *"In whom also we have obtained an inheritance, being predestinated according to the purpose of him who worketh all things after the counsel of his own will."*
> EPHESIANS 1:11

One thing I've noticed is that we as people lack commitment, discipline and consistency; therefore, we sell ourselves short. We don't achieve, nor receive all God has for us. One day while meditating I prayed this prayer: "God my greatest concern is that I never reach my 'there.' I need you to keep me on this earth until I've done what you predestined me to do and I've received all you promised me. Shape and mold me. Take out of me whatever you have to, for me to be in the right position."

We have to stop being so consumed with our own agenda and seek His. That's where true happiness comes from. You may not understand all that's taking place in your life but, as a child of God, you can rest in the truth of His Word that it was predetermined you will succeed. ♥

> *"For I know the thoughts that I think toward you, saith the Lord, thoughts of peace and not of evil, to give you an expected end."*
> JEREMIAH 29:11

God, through this Scripture, gives us the ability to discern (distinguish) when thoughts or situations are not part of His kingdom. We've been given the authority to dismiss and reject them. This is a key Scripture for me in battles against bad doctor reports, financial woes, anything that would seek to steal my peace. When life gets hectic and things are seemingly out of control, we can take comfort in this verse, which assures us, no matter what's going on, that He has our best interest at heart. It's God's desire that we have peace, and experience a blessed, favorable outcome. ♥

For the Mind

> *"Therefore if any man be in Christ, he is a new creature; old things are passed away, behold all things become new."*
> 2 CORINTHIANS 5:17

Old mindsets, hang-ups, habits and issues can no longer hold you captive as you surrender your life to Christ. He makes all things new, as we allow Him to work in our lives. This Scripture worked for me. It explains that I'm not HIV, and HIV is not me. It may be strange to some, but I never identified myself with this label. I viewed it as something trying to attach itself to me. I felt as though it was something outside of me trying to happen to me.

I believe it was God's doing, His way of allowing me to manage the turmoil that goes along with such a label. Even though I went through physical pain at times, and heartache, doctors and medications, it was all just a process, a journey I had to go through. Don't get me wrong; it was extremely difficult, painful at times, and downright impossible for a human to endure alone. However, it wasn't impossible for a supernatural, extraordinary God. ♥

> *"As a man thinketh in his heart
> so is he"*
> PROVERBS 23:7

Whatever issues of your past that try to hold you back, you have permission to be free from their grip on your life. Second Corinthians 5:17 tells us we're no longer bound by our old nature, our old way of thinking or acting. We can have new life in Christ. ♥

› *"Not as though I had already attained, either were already perfect; but I follow after, if that I may apprehend that for which also I am apprehended of Christ Jesus."*
PHILIPPIANS 3:12

I'm sure many people can relate to the inward struggle between wanting things your way and surrendering to God's way. We all have to come to a point in our lives where we seek to fulfill our purpose for being on Planet Earth. Sometimes the purpose may not be desirable in our eyes but to Him it's beautiful.

Some are called to minister to those the world considers "undesirable;" some are called to be millionaires, kings and presidents. We each have a specific purpose and can only be effective when we walk in that purpose.

I don't confess to have arrived. I have a long way to go, but I want to do His will. There are others who feel the same way. You want to live for Him and help others come to know Him and believe in Him for the impossible.

How do we accomplish this task? We must follow Him to obtain that (abundant life, purpose, joy, success…) for which we were apprehended by Christ Jesus. ♥

For the Mind

> *"Casting down imaginations and every high thing that exalteth itself against the knowledge of God, and bringing into captivity every thought to the obedience of Christ."*
> 2 Corinthians 10:5

We must reject those thoughts that come to discourage or discredit our faith. You know: thoughts like, "I'll never make it," "No one wants me," and "I might as well give up." God gave us power to rebuke and denounce these negative thoughts, to take authority over harassing (troublesome, distressing) attacks on our person, in Jesus' name. We can stand in the authority of His name. Keep your thought life in check; if it doesn't line up with the Word of God, dismiss it. Hold fast to that which is good. ♥

For the Soul...

> *"Therefore my beloved, as you have always obeyed, not as in my presence only but now much more in my absence, work out your own salvation with fear and trembling."*
> PHILIPPIANS 2:12 -
> NEW KING JAMES VERSION

It doesn't matter about other people. It matters that you believe, and receive the Word of God for yourself. Don't look on others and their circumstances to dictate your own. Jesus is your healer, your deliverer, your sustainer. Keep your eyes fixed on Jesus. This is an individual walk. People can provide support, wisdom and love as God allows. Nevertheless, when it's all said and done, it matters what you think, and what you believe about your own situation, your relationship and faith in Him. ♥

> *"For it is God which worketh in you both to will and to do of his good pleasure."*
> PHILIPPIANS 2:13

When you allow Him to live in your heart, He works His purpose for your life through you. The good you do, even the very desire to do good, comes from Him. I love this Scripture because it's a reminder that we don't have the power in ourselves, but He in us is all powerful and can accomplish great things. As you yield and surrender your "self" to Him, you allow Him to take pleasure through your life and in turn are blessed because His plans are all good. ♥

For the Soul

*"If the Son therefore shall make you
free, ye shall be free indeed."*
John 8:36

"No holding back, full force ahead, thank you for setting us free, Jesus! Free in Jesus! Open to serve you, to testify of your goodness." Free, meaning not under the control or power of Satan. We're released from captivity; no longer a slave to sin. We're not restrained or in bondage to our past. Jesus has freed us to move forward and achieve our goals. We're free to attain our destiny. You have permission, you're free to be. ♥

> *"Now the Lord is the Spirit, and where the Spirit of the Lord is, there is liberty [emancipation from bondage, freedom]."*
> 2 CORINTHIANS 3:17 - AMPLIFIED VERSION

Is that your cry? You want to be free to just be the person God created you to be. Do you want to not be bound by society and standards other people have set for you? If we look at our lives closely, we can see areas where we're still in bondage, whether it's bondage to our past, our upbringing with old mindsets, bondage to work, to money, or bondage to relationships. This (whatever you're bound by) is an area where we haven't allowed God to be God. Because, as His Word declares, where He is, there is liberty (power to choose, to act and speak freely). Invite Him into your heart, into your life today, that you may be free to be who you were predestined to be. ♥

> *"My son, attend to my words; incline your ear unto my sayings. Let them not depart from your eyes; keep them in the midst of thine heart. For they are life unto those that find them and health to all their flesh."*
> PROVERBS 4:20-24

Scripture is medicine. In one of the darkest times of my life, suffering physically, mentally and spiritually, as I felt life slipping away, I was given the Word of God to stand on. God placed someone in my life to give me a book full of Scriptures pertaining to life and health, to read and meditate on. As I read the Word of God, the pain I'd endured for days on end subsided, and I gained peace of mind and strength to persevere.

The foundation is the Word. When you don't know what to say or what to pray, pray the Word. I am a witness—it works! Nothing and no one was able to bring me out of that dark place, the valley of the shadow of death, but the Word of God. Proverbs 4:20 is just one of many Scriptures I stood on. Just from reading the Scriptures aloud, the vexation (dark, heaviness) in my spirit lifted off me. The Word gives life to those who seek refuge in it.

His Promises...

> *"I can do all things through Christ which strengtheneth me."*
> PHILIPPIANS 4:13

Thank you, Jesus! We can make it. We can do all God destined, all He purposed for us to do in this life through Him. It's His strength, His power working through us. Oh, what peace we'll find when we realize we don't have to do it, do life, all by ourselves. We can rely on the One with all power, all knowledge and all foresight.

It's a joy to rest in the fact that I'm not responsible all by myself to make things happen. If I just have faith, remain God-conscious, pray and trust in Him, I'll accomplish what I'm destined to do. He has placed in us a craving to not become satisfied with the status quo, but to continue to pursue and seek after Him.

As the enemy of our soul speaks defeat in our ears, you know things like: "You can't finish school; you can't have that business," we must not sit by passively and take it. We must speak back to Him with the Word, just as Jesus did in the wilderness (Matthew 4:3-11). Remind the enemy of your soul that you have backup. You will accomplish your goals with God's assistance. And be like David in the Bible (1 Samuel 30:6), who encouraged himself in the Lord, using what he learned by experience. We can make it. We can take it. Yes we can! We can do whatever we need to do in life through Christ. ♥

> *"The thief cometh not, but for to steal,
> and to kill, and to destroy. I am come
> that they might have life, and that they
> might have it more abundantly."*
> JOHN 10:10

It's our enemy the devil's job to discourage us and keep us from the promises of God. He uses things like fear, worry, doubt, shame, regret, deception and people to stop us, to paralyze and immobilize us. He seeks to keep us bound and shackled to the cares of life. From birth to now, the enemy has sought to rob me of my life, to steal my joy and destiny through verbal, sexual and mental abuse. This Scripture lets me know this is not God's plan for my life. It's contrary to His purpose for coming.

When things come to rob you of your joy, your peace or your health, you can know it's not God, because His Word states He came to give us life abundantly. We combat the enemy with the Word of God. Knowledge truly is power. When we know better, we do better. Live life abundantly. ♥

HIS PROMISES

"The Lord is not slack concerning his promise, as some men count slackness; but is longsuffering to us-ward, not willing that any should perish, but that all should come to repentance."
2 PETER 3:9

Things may look or even feel bleak, but this Scripture reminds us that God is faithful. People may promise you things and let you down, sometimes for reasons out of their control. God's not like man. He's not limited. He never fails nor does He break promises. Whatever He has promised you will receive. Sometimes we get in our own way through fear and doubt or trying to work things out ourselves, which leads to trouble. Even with our shortcomings, He's patient with us because He understands us (he created us). So when it gets a little rough, take comfort in this Word that He is faithful and will come through for you. Just hold on, help in on the way. ♥

> *"If we endure hardship,
> we shall reign with him."*
> 2 TIMOTHY 2:12

There will be times of hardship (suffering, pain, loss) living in this world. However, if you go through these things, keeping faith in Jesus (believing He is able to keep you and deliver you out of your situation) you will have the victory. One day you'll rule with Him, having all things in subjection (to have dominion) as He does. Like the Apostle Paul, we're to consider it an honor knowing there's a purpose in our pain. Remember, as you conquer the trials in your life, you're to help others conquer theirs. ♥

> *"We are troubled on every side yet not distressed [in sorrow, or anxiety], we are perplexed [puzzled] but not in despair [giving up hope]. Persecuted [oppressed], but not forsaken, cast down but not destroyed [do away with ruin]."*
> 2 CORINTHIANS 4:8-9

In life, there'll be times where you feel as if all the forces of evil have been unleashed against you, and you want to give up on life and throw in the towel. Maybe you're at this point now. It may seem as though there's no use fighting anymore, there's no hope. I've been at the point of wanting to give up the fight for life.

Let me encourage you. It may surprise you but God knew this time would come and He gave this verse for you to stand on and take strength in knowing a way out was already made, before you ever got in this hard place. You will not be taken out or taken down by the enemy and destroyed. Yes, the day may seem as dark as the night about you right now, but a brighter tomorrow is on its way. ♥

> *"For God has not given us the spirit of fear; but of power, and of love and of a sound mind."*
> 2 TIMOTHY 1:7

Have you ever feared something so much, pondered long and hard and it came to pass? I've done this in times past and, to be honest, I may still get caught in this pattern today if I'm not walking in His Spirit. One minute everything's fine but then I feared getting sick because, "There's something going around," I'm told, and wouldn't you know before too long I'm exhibiting symptoms. Self-fulfilling prophecy they call it in the psychology world.

Another example may be a fear of rejection, that people won't like you. Because you think this way, you may behave in a manner that's defensive or on guard; these actions can cause people to not like you. One thing I feared was mass rejection, when I told my story in the first book I wrote. Instead, I got mass love and support. It's not His will for us to walk around like weaklings with our heads down and with no peace. God desires us to have peace, to be strong in Him and walk in His perfect love. ♥

His Promises

"For we walk by faith, not by sight."
2 Corinthians 5:7

Just because there are some twists and turns with a few steep curves in life doesn't mean the promises of God spoken over your life are no longer so. He hasn't changed His mind. It's at these times you have to remain focused on Him, on His promises, on His Word, despite how foggy or stormy it may get. It's all a façade, designed by the enemy to distract, discourage and detour you. God would never have allowed the storm to happen if you couldn't handle it. The Word of God tells us He won't allow anything you can't handle. He will always provide a way out as you seek Him wholeheartedly. Remember, it's not your strength, but His you're to rely on. As we continue to trust Him, regardless of what we see in front of us, we will obtain victory and all He has promised us. ♥

> *"And we know that all things work
> together for good to them that love God,
> to them who are the called
> according to His purpose."*
> ROMANS 8:28

Not all things that happen in our lives will be good, at first. But turn to God, give the trial, the situation, the relationship to Him, and He will make good come from it. There have been times I've held onto this verse dearly. I spoke to God, saying, "I just don't see it, but your Word says it and I'm going to trust you."

Have you been there? Are you there now? What God wants is for us to not have faith in what we see or feel or hear. In other words, don't rely on our five natural senses but rely on our spiritual sense. Have faith in what you want to see according to His Word and promises. Look forward to the good that will come out of the situation.

You may ask what good can come from losing your job. It may be an opportunity to do what you were meant to do – time to spend with loved ones and foster healthy relationships. I've heard of many testimonies of people who were held up in traffic and ended up avoiding accidents. So, although they may have run late, they were saved from harm. We must learn to be sensitive to God's leading, and to look for the lessons and blessings in everything. ♥

> *"God is not a man, that he should lie;*
> *neither the son of man, that he should*
> *repent: hath he said, and shall he not*
> *do it? Or hath he spoken, and shall*
> *he not make it good?*
> NUMBERS 23:19

God is a promise keeper. He's not like man, going about making empty promises. He doesn't say what He doesn't mean. Take comfort, knowing there's no underlying message or fine print. When God speaks, it is so, just as He has spoken. We don't have to wonder or worry. God keeps His Word. Sometimes you can be bombarded by a series of traumatic events and what He spoke may seem so far away or just not possible. You can come back to this verse and say, despite what's going on, some way, somehow, His Word is coming forth for me. He cannot lie. ♥

> *"Behold I give you power to tread on serpents and scorpions and over all the power of the enemy and nothing shall by any means hurt you."*
> LUKE 10:19

Anyone or anything that would try to come against you as a child of God, one who has accepted Him as Lord, God has given you authority and power to overcome. He in you empowers you to do so. You have the ability within to come out on top. Though you may bear some wounds as you go about this journey (life), you are the victor, and He will cause you to thrive. ♥

> *"God who quickeneth (makes alive) the dead and calleth those things that be not as though they were."*
> ROMANS 4:17

What are the dead things in your life? He has come to call them to life today. Is there a "dead relationship" between mother-daughter, sister-brother, or father-son? Live! Is your financial situation bad? The currency flow stopped? Call it back to life. God has given us the ability to call those things that are not yet manifest to be manifested. He is life, and His desire is that we have life and have it more abundantly in every facet. God first calls the spiritually dead to come alive in Him. When you receive this new life in Him, the chance to experience life in all other areas (emotional, physical, and financial) is available. ♥

> *"But he was wounded for our transgressions, he was bruised for our iniquities: the chastisement of our peace was upon him; and with his stripes we are healed."*
> ISAIAH 53:5

He, Jesus, was wounded (suffered, injured) for our misbehavior, our violations in our lives. You may say, "But I didn't do anything wrong." From the beginning of time, mankind was in a fallen state due to the sins of our forefather Adam. It was necessary, according to law, that the sins be paid for by sacrifice and the shedding of blood. The only one able to pay for sin once and for all was the perfect Lamb, the Son of God, Jesus Christ. He offered Himself at Calvary, was beaten and hung on a cross so you and I could be free. He did this so we can have healing and deliverance from that sinful nature, and all the harmful things that go with it. ♥

> *"Greater is he that is in you,*
> *than he that is in the world."*
> 1 JOHN 4:4

You must remind yourself that God is greater and bigger than whatever you may face. The enemy is of this world, but you have access to the One who created this world. That should encourage you and increase your faith. God has created a pathway (Jesus) through His Son for us to have fellowship with Him. We can have an intimate relationship with the Father. He longs to call us friends. He will back His friends always. When you're pressed and the victory appears unattainable, grip this Word, and remind yourself, the size of the problem is no match for your God. ♥

His Promises

> *"For this purpose the Son of God was manifested, that he might destroy the works of the devil."*
> 1 John 3:8

Jesus came to destroy the works of the devil. What does that mean? It means sin, evil, wickedness, sickness, poverty, and so on. When we're hit with these things, we must take note that they're not of God. He sent His Son to annihilate these things, so as to give us authority over them. You don't have to allow these things to consume you and take you out. Jesus defeated the works of the devil at Calvary's cross.

So when I came to moments in my life where it seemed the entire underworld was breaking loose, because I suffered on every side: without money; house in chaos; emotional and mental turmoil; and physical pain; I would confess (speak) this Scripture and remind myself that the battle has already been won. You can do the same. ♥

> *"I shall live and not die to declare the
> works of the Lord."*
> PSALM 118:17

We can have challenges with our health that look, feel and sound grave, but for God. I've been diagnosed with what's considered a terminal illness. One of the lessons I learned during these times of feeling I was going to die is that things aren't always what they appear to be. The enemy does his best to magnify the negative and create doubt and fear.

The opposite of fear is faith. Be assured that you can confess His Word and triumph over the enemy, over sickness, over disease, over pain. It's at these moments that you must reflect on what God has already done for you. Reflect on the trials He brought you through and remind yourself that He's the same God. If He did it then, He'll do it now.

I once heard a testimony of a mother whose son went on a church camping trip. The bus crashed and caught fire; at the scene, her son was basically given no chance of survival. This mother saw how horrible the situation appeared but stood on God's Word, day after day, that he'd live, despite setbacks. Today, her son is alive because his mom refused to give up on him and spoke God's Word over him unswervingly. The doctors call it a miracle. We agree.

If you need inspiration, if you need examples of Him bringing people out of grim situations, read your Bible. It's full of healing and deliverance testimonies. ♥

PRAISE

PRAISE

> *"In everything give thanks for this is the will of God in Christ Jesus concerning you."*
> 1 THESSALONIANS 5:18

At one of the most traumatic times in my life, when darkness covered me and the pangs of death encompassed me, I felt like giving up the fight for my life, for the promises of God. Then the Spirit of God prompted me to create a list of everything for which to be thankful. So someway, somehow, in this surround sound of pain, I reached into my heart to compose a list of the blessings I'd received from God. It went like this:

- Physically: I may not be what I'd like to be, but I'm blessed.
- Financially: I may be in some debt, but I have a roof over my head, a job and reliable transportation.
- Socially: I may be lonely at times, but I have good friends and family who love and support me.
- Spiritually: I may feel stuck, but I'm saved. I've been anointed for a work, and He is working in me to bring out the best.

The list was several pages long. By the time I finished, I was encouraged to push pass the pain and disappointments of life and expect brighter days ahead. I spoke out the Scripture that He inhabits the praises of His people, those who have accepted him as Lord, He dwells, hangs around in the midst of their praise (Psalms 22:3). Those words became real to me; I was living them.

When you give thanks for all He has done, you can't help but feel empowered and encouraged. You realize He's the same God who brought you through before, and will do it again. ♥

PRAISE

*"Let everything that have breath
praise ye the Lord"*
PSALMS 150:6

One important key weapon in this fight of faith is *praise*! It's so very powerful. As one song states; "When praises go up, blessings come down." God inhabits the praises of His people (those who receive Him as Lord). Praise is a sacrifice. When we praise, we're doing something our flesh wouldn't normally do and may be uncomfortable doing at first. It can take many forms: singing, dancing, shouting, waving our hands.

We were created to praise Him. He's worthy of all praise. I know without a shadow of a doubt that my praise has been instrumental in keeping me together, in the fight of faith. There are stories in the Bible that exhibit the power of praise. Paul and Silas, who were in jail, praised and prayed unto God and were miraculously set free Acts 16:25-34). There's a Scripture, Nehemiah 8:10, that states: "The joy of the Lord is my strength." Praising God actually produces strength, strength to persevere and obtain the promise of God.

Are you going to praise Him? Try it, and see for yourself. ♥

PRAISE

"And they overcame him by the blood of the Lamb and by the word of their testimony; and they loved not their life unto the death."
REVELATION 12:11

We exhibit our faith when testifying about God's goodness. In turn, it can free us from the bondage of keeping secrets, all while giving Him glory and encouraging someone who may be going through similar challenges. ♥

THE WORD

The Word

"There is no fear in love. But perfect love drives out fear, because fear has to do with punishment. The one who fears is not made perfect in love."
1 John 4:18 –
New International Version

"Make me perfect in love, O God, according to your Word." As easy and simple as the verse sounds, it can be a challenge to rest in His perfect love and not fear anything. In this world, there are some frightful things happening almost every minute. So how can we not fear? I've come to the conclusion that as we develop an intimate relationship with Jesus, we learn of His character and His nature. The closer we get to Him, the fear fades. We come to know Him and trust Him as our God, our protector. ♥

> *"O Lord, thou hast searched me and known me."*
> PSALM 139

Have you ever come to a point where you questioned who you are? This verse affirms that though you may not know who you are and have times of confusion, He knows. Situations can actually get so hectic that you feel lost and don't understand anything anymore. God gave us Psalm 139 in its entirety to encourage us that He is aware at all times where we are and what's going on with us. He created us, and He understands even when we don't. We have to trust Him to bring us through those times of uncertainty. You have to go within yourself in prayer and meditation to find the answers to your questions. He has the answers and is ready to give them to you as you search diligently for them.

There's a young woman I read about who shared that, growing up, she found herself in deep depression and suffering from low self-esteem. She learned to read God's Word and apply it to her life, which pulled her out of the depression. She read that she was fearfully and wonderfully made. Today, she's a successful single mom on the move, inspiring other young women to find their worth in Christ. ♥

www.ingramcontent.com/pod-product-compliance
Lightning Source LLC
Chambersburg PA
CBHW070501050426
42449CB00012B/3073